Tl

The Tiny Book of Dirty Jokes

Mr J

HarperCollins*Publishers*

HarperCollins*Publishers*
77–85 Fulham Palace Road,
Hammersmith, London W6 8JB

www.**fire**and**water**.com

This paperback edition 2000
1 3 5 7 9 8 6 4 2

Previously published in Great Britain
by Angus & Robertson 1982

ISBN 0 00 710498 7

Set in Stone Sans by Rowland Phototypesetting Ltd,
Bury St Edmunds, Suffolk
Printed and bound in Great Britain by Scotprint

An old man made it shakily through the door to the Mustang Ranch, outside Reno, Nevada.

The receptionist stared at him. 'You gotta be in the wrong place,' she exclaimed.

'Ain't this where you allus got forty-five girls ready 'n' able?'

The woman looked perplexed. 'Ready for what?'

'I want a girl,' the old man rasped.

'How old are you, Pop?' she asked.

'Ninety-two,' he replied.

'Ninety-two? Pop, you've *had* it!'

'Oh,' said the old man, a little disconcerted as his trembling fingers reached for his wallet. 'How much do I owe you?'

Aventriloquist was driving in the country when he was attracted to a large farm. He asked for and was given a tour.

As he was shown through the barn, the ventriloquist thought he'd have some fun. He proceeded to make one of the horses talk.

The hired hand, wide-eyed with fear, rushed from the barn to the farmer. 'Sam,' he shouted, 'those animals are talking! If that little sheep says anything about me, it's a damned lie!'

The salesman asked at a farm for a room for the night. The farmer told him there was no space.

'I could let you sleep with my daughter,' the farmer said, 'if you promise not to bother her.'

The salesman agreed.

After supper, he was led to the room. He undressed in the dark, slipped into bed, and felt the farmer's daughter at his side.

The next morning he asked for his bill.

'It'll be just five dollars, since you had to share,' the farmer said.

'Your daughter was very cold,' the salesman said.

'Yes, I know,' said the farmer. 'We're going to bury her today.'

Little William went to his father and said, 'Daddy, where did I come from?'

The father started to stutter and stammer, but he realized that he had to tell his son the facts of life.

'Sit down, Willie,' he said.

At great length, he described the whole business of creation, beginning with the birds and the bees. Then he went into the most graphic descriptions of human intercourse.

He concluded at last, feeling limp and drained. 'Okay, Willie, do you understand now?'

Willie scratched his head. 'Not really, Dad. Henry says he came from Bournemouth but you haven't told me where I come from.'

The Greek ship owner, Ori Oristotle, was having a house built. He said to the architect, 'Don't disturb that tree over there because that is where I had my first sex.'

'How sentimental, Mr Oristotle,' the architect said.

'Yes,' continued Ori Oristotle, 'And don't touch that tree over there either. Because that's where her mother stood watching.'

'Her mother just stood there while you were fucking her daughter?' the architect asked.

'Yes,' said the Greek ship owner.

'But, Mr Oristotle, what did her mother say?'

'Baaa.'

A drunk walked into a bar crying. One of the other men at the bar asked him what happened.

'I did a horrible thing,' sniffled the drunk. 'Just a few hours ago I sold my wife to someone for a bottle of scotch.'

'That *is* awful,' said the other guy. 'And now she's gone and you want her back, right?'

'Right,' said the drunk, still crying.

'You're sorry you sold her because you realized too late that you love her, right?'

'Oh, no,' said the drunk. 'I want her back because I'm thirsty again!'

The Frenchman and the Italian were in the woods hunting together when suddenly a voluptuous blonde girl raced across their path, totally nude.

'Would I love to eat that? *Oui, oui!*' the Frenchman said, smacking his lips.

So the Italian shot her.

She was wearing a very tight skirt, and when she tried to board the bus she found she couldn't lift her leg. She reached back and unzipped her zipper. It didn't seem to do any good, so she reached back and unzipped it again.

Suddenly the man behind her lifted her up and put her on the top step.

'How dare you?' she demanded.

'Well, lady,' he said, 'by the time you unzipped my fly for the second time I thought we were good friends.'

The little boy was sitting on the curb crying and an old man who was passing by came over to him.

'What's the matter, little boy?' he asked. 'Why are you crying?'

The little boys said, 'I'm crying because I can't do what the big boys do.'

The old man sat down on the curb and cried too.

It was his wedding night and the minister finished undressing in the bathroom and walked into the bedroom. He was surprised to see that his bride had already slipped between the bed sheets.

'My dear,' he said, 'I thought I would find you on your knees.'

She said, 'Well, honey, I can do it that way too, but it gives me the hiccoughs.'

Four men had played golf together for two years. At the conclusion of the games, three of the men always showered together, then had a few drinks at the bar. The fourth man would hurry home.

One day one of the trio asked the fourth man, 'Listen, how come you never stick around?'

The fourth man was uncomfortable. 'All right, I'll tell you. I don't stay because I don't want to shower with you. I'm embarrassed because my penis is very small.'

The other man asked, 'Does it work?'

'Sure, it works very well.'

'Well how would you like to trade it in for one that looks good in the shower?'

The husband kissed his wife goodbye and got into his Cadillac to drive to work in New York City. He'd gone about a mile when he remembered that he'd left something in the bedroom. So he turned the car around and drove back home.

When he walked into the bedroom, there was his wife, lying totally nude on the bed and the milkman standing totally nude beside her.

The milkman promptly went into a squatting position on the rug and said, 'I'm glad you're here, Mr Jones, because I was just telling your wife that if she doesn't pay the milk bill, I'm gonna shit all over the floor.'

The Mother Superior in the convent school was chatting with her young charges and she asked them what they wanted to be when they grew up.

A twelve-year-old said, 'I want to be a prostitute.'

The Mother Superior fainted dead away on the spot. When they revived her, she raised her head from the ground and gasped, 'What–did–you–say?'

The young girl shrugged. 'I said I want to be a prostitute.'

'A prostitute!' the Mother Superior said, 'Oh, praise sweet Jesus! And I thought you said you wanted to be a Protestant.'

The judge came home and found his wife in bed with his very best friend.

'Hey, what do you think you're doing?'

'See,' the wife said to the man beside her, 'I told you he was stupid.'

Little Jimmy had become a real nuisance while the men tried to concentrate on their poker game. The youngster insisted on running behind the players and calling out the cards they held, until the players became so annoyed that they threatened to quit. At this point, the boy's uncle took Jimmy and led him away. The uncle returned in a short time without Jimmy and the game resumed.

For the balance of the afternoon, there was no trouble from Jimmy. After the game had ended and the players were settling up, one of the men asked Jimmy's uncle, 'What in the world did you do to Jimmy?'

'Not much,' the boy's uncle replied. 'I showed him how to jerk off.'

A reporter asked the great artist Picasso why he tolerated the sexual escapades of his much younger wife.

'Well,' said the artist, 'I'd rather have 20% of a growing concern than a 100% interest in a bankruptcy.'

The aged patient toddered into the doctor's office
with a serious complaint.

'Doc, you've got to do something to lower my
sex drive.'

'Come on now, Mr Peters,' the doctor said,
'your sex drive's all in your head.'

'That's what I mean' you've got to lower it a
little.'

Not in Webster's Dictionary: Definition of a gynaecologist as a spreader of old wives' tales.

Overheard at a cocktail party: A husband was asking his wife, 'Tell me, dear, before we married, did you say you were oversexed or over sex?'

Two buddies at the bar, drinking away, were comparing the sexual behaviour of their spouses.

'Hey,' one asked, 'does your wife close her eyes when you're pumping away on her?'

'She sure does,' replied the other. 'She just can't stand to watch me having a good time.'

An important executive was telling friends at his country club about some of his experiences. 'So I bought this yacht that could carry fifty people and I took it out for a maiden voyage and it hit a reef and sunk.

'Then I bought an airplane and on the first flight it hit another plane on the field and it burned up.

'Then I married this beautiful blonde and no sooner did I get home that I found her fooling around with the chauffeur and I had to divorce her.'

'So what's the moral?' one of the others asked.

'Clear as a bell,' said the old man. 'If it swims, flies or fucks, lease it, don't buy it.'

It's a business doing pleasure with you,' said the whore as she accepted her payment.

The bride-to-be and her best friend were discussing the former's impending wedding.

'If you want an unforgettable wedding night,' her friend said, 'get him to eat a dozen oysters after the ceremony.'

A week later the new bride thanked her friend but said plaintively, 'Only eight of the oysters worked.'

What is the meaning of the word 'indecent'? When it's firm and long and thrust to the hilt, then it's indecent.

Three words guaranteed to destroy any man's ego: 'Is it in?'

Two kids were having the standard argument about whose father could beat up whose father.

One boy said, 'My father is better than your father.'

The other kid said, 'Well, my mother is better than your mother.'

The first boy paused, 'I guess you're right. My father says the same thing.'

An old gentleman slowly approached the local brothel and pressed the doorbell.

The madam opened the door, looked at the old fellow with a critical eye and then asked: 'What can we do for you, sir?'

'I need a girl,' the senior citizen said.

'For you, the charge is a hundred dollars.'

'You're putting me on,' he exclaimed.

'That will be an extra ten dollars,' said the madam.

Two men sitting side by side were having their respective scalps tonsured. The first barber asked his client if he'd like some French toilet water on his hair.

'Oh, no,' the man said. 'My wife would think I'd been in a French whorehouse.'

The second barber asked the same question of his client, who said, 'Why, sure, my wife has never been in a French whorehouse.'

It was the first Christmas and the first of the Three Wise Men slowly approached the barn and gingerly crossed over the threshold – into a big juicy pile of horse shit.

Looking down at his gold slippers, he let out a shriek – 'Je-sus Christ!'

The woman at the manger turned to her companion and said, 'Joseph, that's a better name for the kid than Irving.'

The henpecked husband was asked why he couldn't bear to sit through porno movies.

'I can't stand one guy enjoying himself more in ten minutes than I have in the last twenty years.'

The tough character was mumbling to his friend. 'My girl, Mary, is going to die of syphilis.'

'No,' the friend said, 'people don't die of syphilis anymore.'

'They do when they give it to me!' was the rejoinder.

So this old man went to his doctor.

'I've got toilet problems,' he complained.

'Well, let's see. How is your urination?'

'Every morning at seven o'clock like a baby.'

'Good. How about your bowel movement?'

'Eight o'clock each morning like clockwork.'

'So what's the problem?' the doctor asked.

'I don't wake up until nine!'

Through the first four holes in the golf course, Jim was very quiet. Finally, on the fifth tee, John asked, 'What the hell's the matter, Jim? You're so silent.'

'It's my wife, Ann,' John replied. 'Ever since she's been working overtime at the phone company, she's cut our sex down to twice a week.'

'You're lucky,' replied John. 'She's cut me off completely.'

A young man in love with a girl he wanted to sleep with was so ashamed of his small penis that he was afraid of bringing up the question, or of letting her see him naked.

One dark night he drove her around in his car and parked in a dark lane. As they kissed he surreptitiously opened his fly and put his weapon in her hand.

'Thanks,' she said. 'But you know I don't smoke.'

A patient, suffering from an impacted wisdom tooth, went to his dentist.

'That tooth has got to be pulled immediately,' the dentist said as he reached for a wicked-looking set of forceps.

The patient reached out and got a tight grip on the dentist's balls. 'We're not going to hurt each other, are we, doctor?'

The census taker asked a girl to give her occupation.

'Whore,' she answered.

'I can't list it that way, Miss.'

'Okay, put down prostitute.'

'I can't list it that way either.'

'How about chicken raiser?'

'Chicken raiser?' he asked in puzzlement.

'Sure, last year I raised nine hundred cocks.'

The white missionary had lived in peace in the African village for more than a year but now the tribal Chief approached him.

'What is it, Chief?' he asked.

'You in big trouble,' the Chief said. 'Yesterday white baby was born to my cousin. You only white man in village. We probably roast you alive.'

'Look, old man,' The missionary said. 'I know it looks bad. But you see that flock of white sheep?'

'I see 'em.'

'Then notice that black sheep in the flock. It's the only one and there are no other black sheep in the village.'

'Okay, okay,' said the Chief hastily. 'You no tell and I no tell.'

Charlie was telling his tale of woe to his boss. He said, 'I was so drunk last night that I don't know how I got home. Not realizing it was my bed I slept in when I awoke. I handed the woman next to me a £20 bill.'

'Is that what's making you sad?'

'No,' said Charlie. 'It was my wife I gave the £20 to, but she gave me £10 change.'

A nosy neighbour remonstrated with the woman in the adjourning apartment. 'Mrs Smith, do you think it right that this seventeen-year-old boy spends three hours every night in your apartment?'

Mrs Smith replied, 'It's a platonic friendship. It's play for him and a tonic for me.'

The gynaecologist told the young woman on his examination table. 'Go home and tell you husband to prepare for a baby.'

'But I don't have a husband,' the girl replied.

'Then, go home and tell your lover.'

'But I don't have a lover. I've never had a lover!'

'In that case,' the doctor sighed, 'go home and tell your mother to prepare for the second coming of Christ.'

On an isolated part of a beach, a young boy and girl were teasing each other. They were boasting about how one had more than the other of everything.

The nine-year-old boy figured out a way to win the contest. He removed his swim trunks and said, 'See, here's something you don't have.'

The little girl ran away and returned a few minutes later. She pulled down the bottom of her bathing suit. 'My mummy says that with one of these, I can get as many of those as I want.'

A guy walked into the confessional booth and confessed to the priest, 'Father, I got laid ten times today!'

The shocked priest exclaimed, 'What kind of Catholic are you?'

'I'm not a Catholic at all . . . but I had to tell someone!'

A tour bus travelling through northern Nevada paused briefly at the Mustang Ranch, near Sparks. The guide noted: 'We are now passing the largest house of prostitution in America.'

A male passenger piped up: 'Why?'

Alex came home from a business trip and found his daughter Rose crying bitterly.

'What's the matter, darling?' asked Alex.

'Mummy almost died last night,' sobbed Rose.

'That's nonsense,' said the father. 'Why do you say that?'

'Well,' said Rose, 'you always told us that when we die we'll see God; so when I heard Mummy moaning last night I rushed to her bedroom and she was screaming, "Oh God, here I come," and she would have but Uncle Jerry held her down.'

A young nun said to her Mother Superior:
'I was out walking in the garden last night and the gardener took me, threw me to the ground and, well, you know . . . Can you give me penance?'

'Go and eat ten lemons,' said the Mother Superior.

'But that won't cleanse my sins away.'

'I know, but it will wipe that contented grin off your face.'

An American, an Englishman, and a Frenchman were discussing a good example of savoir-faire. 'Well,' said the American, 'if you came home and found your wife in bed with another man and you didn't kill the son of a bitch, that to me is savoir-faire.'

'Not quite, chaps,' said the Englishman. 'If you came home and found your wife in bed with another man and you said, "Please, sir, carry on," that's savoir-faire.'

'Mais non,' said the Frenchman. 'If you came home and found your wife in bed with another man and you said, "Please, sir, carry on" and the man was able to continue, *he's* got savoir-faire!'

On a town beside an Indian reservation a beautiful Indian girl was soliciting business, when a prospect asked her rate.

'One hundred dollars!' he exclaimed. 'Why, the Indians sold Manhattan for only twenty-four dollars.'

'Could be,' she smiled and wiggled her hips. 'But Manhattan just lies there.'

A seventy-five-year-old gentleman visited his doctor to complain about his impotency.

'Why me?' he grumbled. 'I have a friend eighty years old who says that he –'

The doctor interrupted: 'You can *say* too!'

An eminent teacher and thinker once expressed his philosophy of life succinctly. 'When it all boils down to the essence of truth,' the philosopher said, 'one must live by a dog's rule of life: If you can't eat it or fuck it, piss on it!'

The young farm helper was telling his friend about his wedding night.

'Boy, was my girl dumb! She put a pillow under her ass instead of her head.'

A father was talking to his son just before the son's marriage, explaining what the son could be looking forward to in his marriage.

He said, 'Son, in the very beginning, it's tri-weekly. After you've been married ten years or so, it's try weekly. But then after your silver anniversary, it's try weakly.'

What did the Polack do with his first fifty-cent piece? He married her.

And then there's the little boy who got up at midnight to go to the bathroom and passed his parents' bedroom. Noticing that the door was opened, he walked in and saw his mother performing fellatio on his father.

The boy walked out of the bedroom scratching his head and muttering, 'And they sent *me* to the doctor for sucking my thumb!'

A businessman returned home from the office with some startling gossip. He informed his wife that he'd heard that their neighbour in apartment 4-G had fucked every woman in the building except one.

'That's right,' replied the wife. 'It's that stuck-up Mrs Cohen on the eighth floor!'

The parlourmaid in the home of a famous acting family was openly desired and admired by the nineteen-year-old son of the household. He schemed and schemed but could think of no way to get the young woman into his bed.

Finally, one evening, opportunity presented itself and he persuaded the young miss to join him between the sheets. Much to his despair and chagrin, his weapon refused to come to attention.

'Don't feel too bad,' the parlourmaid said. 'The same thing often happens to your father.'

John had two pet monkeys whom he loved very much, but both died within two days of each other. He decided to take their bodies to the taxidermist so that they would be with him forever. The taxidermist gave him an estimate for the job and asked if he wanted them mounted.

'No,' came the reply. 'Just have them shaking hands.'

A bosomy blonde was trying on an extremely low cut dress. As she studied herself in the mirror, she asked the saleswoman if she thought it was too low-cut.

'Do you have hair on your chest?' the saleswoman asked.

'No!'

'Then,' the saleswoman said, 'it's too low-cut!'

When queried by his best friend about the joys of his recent marriage, the young bridegroom shook his head disconsolately.

'I'm not sure,' he muttered. 'When I planned marriage I had dreams of a girl who'd be a lady in the streets, a great cook in the kitchen, and a whore in bed. And what do I have? A whore in the streets, a lady in the bedroom, and a great cook . . . never!'

A comely young blonde was telling her friend at a cocktail party that she was off men for life. 'They lie, they cheat, they are just no good. From now on, when I want sex I'll use my vibrator.'

'But what if the batteries run out? What will you do?' asked the friend.

'Just what I do with my boyfriend – I'll fake an orgasm.'

Giovanni lived in Palermo, Italy. One day he arrived from work early, to find his wife in bed with Pietro, the butcher.

The wife screamed; Pietro screamed.

Meanwhile, Giovanni ran to the closet, pulled out a pistol, and faced his wife.

He put the barrel of the pistol to his forehead and smirked at her: 'Don't feel sorry for me, you bitch. You're gonna be next!'

George took his girlfriend to bed for the first time. He was working away very hard, but she was not responding at all. Finally, in exasperation, he asked her, 'What's the matter?'

She said: 'It's your organ. I don't think it's big enough.'

To which George replied, 'Well, I didn't think I'd be playing in a cathedral!'

Jones, returning from a business trip, was surprised to find his wife in bed with a strange man.

'Why, you rotten bastard!' the husband exploded.

'Wait, darling,' said Mrs Jones. 'You know that fur coat I got last winter? This man gave it to me. Remember the diamond necklace you like so much? This man gave it to me. And remember when you couldn't afford a second car and I got a Toyota? This man gave it to me.'

'For heaven's sake, it's drafty here!' shouted the husband 'Cover him so he doesn't catch cold!'

A wealthy Jewish lawyer was unhappy over the romantic pursuits of his junior-college son. He told his closest friend, 'My son's a homosexual.' But then he added, 'The situation could be worse, though. He's in love with a doctor.'

The recruits for the college football team were lined up to take their first physical before the new coach and, of course, were stripped naked. Charlie, the candidate for the tight end job, stepped before the coach, who was amazed to see that Charlie's cock was about sixteen inches long but only half an inch thick.

The coach exclaimed, 'Charlie, what the hell happened to you?'

Charlie explained, 'Listen, I was nineteen years old before I found out you weren't supposed to roll it between your hands.'

Stan did a hitch in the navy, which kept him away for eighteen months, during which his beautiful young wife sat at home awaiting his return.

On the first day of his leave she spied him entering their apartment house and quickly ran to the bedroom, throwing off all her clothes. She sat there breathlessly until she heard Stan's heavy knocking at the door.

'Darling,' she yelled as she ran to fling it open, 'I know why you're knocking.'

'Yes,' he gasped, 'but do you know what I'm knocking with?'

John took his new girl to the movies, which they both enjoyed. After the show he asked what she wanted to do. 'I want to get weighed,' she said.

He took her to the drugstore, where the machine said her weight was 107 pounds.

Afterwards, she pouted and sulked for the rest of the evening.

When John finally escorted her home, he tried to kiss her at the door, but she pushed him away, saying, 'Go on home. I had a wowsy time.'

A bishop bought two parrots and taught them to say the rosary. He even had two sets of tiny rosary beads made for them.

After months of exhaustive training, the parrots were able to recite the rosary and use the beads at the same time. The bishop was so pleased that he decided to teach another parrot the rosary. He went to the pet store and bought a female parrot, which he brought home and put into the cage with the other two.

As he did this, one parrot turned to the other and said, 'Throw away your beads, George – our prayers have been answered!'

The customer in a bordello was dismayed to see the unshaven armpits of the hooker as she undressed.

'So much wool, so much wool!' he muttered.

As she slipped off her panties, he noticed another prodigious growth.

'So much wool, so much wool!' he exclaimed again.

The girl retorted, 'Look, mister, did you come here to get laid or to knit?'

Girl in cinema: 'The man next to me is masturbating!'

Girlfriend: 'Ignore him.'

'I can't; he's using my hand!'

How do porcupines make love? V-e-r-y carefully!

Not in Mother Goose Rhymes:

> Y stands for Yanker,
> The self-driving chap.
> He greases his pole and
> Provokes his own sap.
>
> Absolved of the need of
> A quarrelsome wife,
> He humps himself nightly
> And lives a great life.

Morris left for a two-day business trip to Chicago. He was only a few blocks from his house, when he realized that he had left the airplane tickets on his bureau top. He returned and quietly entered the house. His wife, in her skimpiest negligee, was standing at the sink washing the breakfast dishes.

She looked so inviting that he tiptoed up behind her, reached out, and squeezed her left tit.

'Leave only one quart of milk,' she said. 'Morris won't be here for breakfast tomorrow.'

After General Custer's troops had left to return to the fort, the Indian chief called his tribe together and said, 'I must report on the battle. There is good news and there is bad news. The bad news is that we were soundly trounced by the American troopers. They burned down our camp, raped our women, and took our food supplies. We'll have nothing to eat throughout this cold winter except buffalo turds.'

The chief's son piped up: 'If that's the bad news, what's the good news?'

The chief said, 'There are plenty of buffalo out here.'

The new husband, a Cockney stagehand, had a most satisfactory nuptial night with his young bride. Forgetting his marital state he quickly dressed himself, threw several coins on the bureau, and headed for the door. On the way out he recalled his new status and returned to his bride. There he found her biting on the coins in an experienced manner.

She snuggled up to him and murmured, 'I'm yours for the asking . . . I'm asking fifty dollars.'

The attractive wife told her husband she was going on vacation with a girlfriend, but she really went with her long-time wealthy lover, who gave her a beautiful $7,500 mink coat. But she couldn't bring it home so she figured a way. She pawned the mink coat.

She came home and told her husband she had found a pawn ticket, which was really the pawn ticket to her mink coat; and she asked her husband to find out what had been pawned.

Her husband returned and told his wife it was just a cheap watch. The next day his secretary was wearing a $7,500 mink coat.

A stately-looking matron was walking through the Bronx Zoo, studying the animals. When she passed the porcupine enclosure she beckoned to a nearby attendant.

'Young man,' she began, 'do the North American porcupines have sharper pricks than those raised in Africa?'

The attendant thought a moment. 'Well, ma'am,' he answered, 'the African porcupine's quills are sharper . . . but I think their pricks are about the same.'

A kindly young woman saw a little boy standing on a street curb attempting to relieve himself. Giving in to her maternal instincts, the woman helped the lad release his organ from his pants. She evinced considerable surprise when the organ proved to be a man-sized tool, growing in her hand as the lad sighed with relief. 'How old are you, little man?' she asked.

'Thirty-three, ma'am,' answered the pint-sized jockey.

'Papa,' said the farmer's son, 'you were a sheep-herder in your younger days; perhaps you can tell me where virgin wool comes from.'

'Virgin wool, my son, comes from the sheep the herders couldn't catch.'

Girls who use their heads can stop the population explosion.

A whore's customer, deciding to leave without payment, yelled at the supine lady, 'If it's a girl, call it Fatima.'

'Fine,' said the whore, 'and if it's an itch, you call it eczema!'

A concerned patient visited his physician and asked him if masturbation was harmful.

'No,' the doctor said. 'Not if you don't do it too often.'

'How about three times a day?'

'That seems a little excessive. Why don't you get yourself a girl?'

'I've got a girl,' the patient said.

'I mean a girl you can live with and sleep with.'

'I've got one like that.'

'Then why in heaven's name do you masturbate three times a day?'

'Oh,' said the patient disgustedly, 'she doesn't like it during mealtimes.'

A guy had his male cat 'fixed' because he was a menace to the neighbourhood, sneaking out at night and impregnating all the neighbours' female cats.

The tom still sneaks out at night . . . but now he acts as consultant.

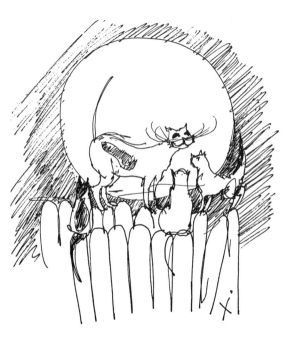

Inflation was getting out of hand so Joe suggested to his wife, Louise, that they try a unique way to save some money on the side.

'Every time I lay you, I'll give you a dollar for your piggy bank,' he said.

A few weeks later, they decided to open the piggy bank. Out tumbled a bunch of dollars, but these were mixed with a rich cluster of fives, tens and twenties.

'Louise,' asked Joe, where did you get all that money? Each time we fucked I only gave you a dollar.'

'So?' she said. 'Do you think everyone is as stingy as you?'

A man took his wife to the theatre. During the interval, he had to urinate in the worst way. He hurried to the back and searched in vain for the men's room.

At last he came upon a fountain surrounded by pretty foliage. He realized that he had wandered backstage. Noting that no one was around, and in desperation, he pissed into the fountain.

He had difficulty finding his way back to the auditorium, and by the time he sat down next to his wife, the curtain was up and actors were moving about on the stage.

'Did I miss much of the second act?' he whispered.

'Miss it?' she said, 'You were in it!'

'Do you know the difference between a cocksucker and a corned beef sandwich?'

'No.'

'Good. Come over tomorrow for lunch.'

Three nuns were walking along the street and one was describing with her hands the tremendous grapefruit she'd seen in Florida.

The second one, also with her hands, described the huge bananas she's seen in Jamaica.

The third nun, a little deaf, asked, 'Father who?'

A man was standing on a train platform seeing the train off and he observed someone near him shouting at one of the departing passengers, 'Goodbye. Your wife was a great lay! Your wife was a great lay!'

He was stunned.

After the train pulled away, he walked over to the man who'd done the shouting, and asked, 'Did I hear you correctly? Did you tell that man his wife was a great lay?'

The other man shrugged his shoulders. 'It isn't really true,' he said, 'but I don't want to hurt his feelings.'

Farmer Brown had been screwing one of his pigs for four years, when he was suddenly hit by pangs of conscience. It tortured him so much that he decided to tell the priest about it in confession.

The priest was shocked and could only say to Farmer Brown, 'Well, tell me, was the pig a male or a female?'

'A female, of course,' said Farmer Brown. 'What do you think I am – some sort of a queer?'

The delegate from Africa was in Moscow, and saw a game of Russian roulette: someone put the barrel of a pistol to his head and pulled the trigger. One of the six chambers contained a real bullet.

Now the Russian delegate was visiting the African nation.

'We would like to show you African roulette,' the Ambassador said.

'How do you play it?'

The Ambassador pointed to six buxom African girls. 'Any of these girls will give you a blow job.'

'Where is the roulette part? Where is the jeopardy?' the Russian asked.

'Well, one of the girls is a cannibal.'

Two couples who had been great friends for years decided to share a holiday.

They pitched two tents and cooked their dinners over a roaring campfire. Ample supplies of booze made the food tastier.

When it came bedtime, one of the men asked the other three: 'What do you think of all this switching around that's going on?'

The question excited the others, and they decided to experiment.

After a few hours, the man turned to his new bedmate and said, 'I haven't had such a great time in years. Do you think the girls are having as much fun as we are?'

An inexperienced young man, prior to his wedding, asked his father how to conduct himself.

'Well,' said the father, 'you take the thing you used to play with when you were a teenager and put it where you wife wee-wees.'

So the young man took his baseball and threw it in the toilet.

An airplane passenger, being served drinks by the stewardess, exclaimed: 'Hey, here's something new . . . an ice cube with a hole in it!'

'What's new about that?' answered the man sitting alongside. 'I married one.'

The on-the-make young executive drinking at the bar was taken aback when the pretty office worker he propositioned snapped at him: 'No, buster, you've got the words "liberated" and "free" mixed up!'

A travelling salesman, completing a trip earlier than anticipated, sent his wife a telegram: 'Returning home Friday.'

Arriving home, he found his wife in bed with another man. Being a person of non-violence, he complained to his father-in-law, who said, 'I'm sure there must be an explanation.'

The next day the father-in-law was all smiles. 'I knew there was an explanation. She didn't get your telegram.'

First Drunk: 'My wife is an angel.'

Second Drunk: 'You're lucky . . . my wife is still alive!'

A man and his attractive companion were enjoying a cocktail party where one of the other female guests was expounding her philosophy. 'I guess I'm just a animal,' she was saying, 'all I want to do is sleep and make love.' The man's companion agreed, 'I sleep and make love too.'

'Yes,' the man said, 'but do you do both at the same time!'

Little Gwen opened the back door to the kitchen where her mother was cooking dinner.

'Mom,' she asked, 'can a nine-year-old girl become pregnant?'

'Of course not,' her mother said.

Gwen turned around. 'Okay, fellows,' she called, 'let's continue playing the game.'

A young student, very pretty and sexy, wore an extra tight blouse and skirt which magnified her abundant charms.

She wriggled up to her professor after class and cooed: 'Professor, I'd do anything to pass your exam with high marks.'

The professor smiled at her, 'Anything?'

'Yes, anything . . .'

'Okay,' the professor said. 'Study!'

An armless man walked into John's Bar and ordered a beer. When served, he asked the bartender to help him drink it by holding the glass. This was done cheerfully and then repeated twice. After the third beer, the customer asked the location of the men's room. The bartender pointed to the rear of the bar but intoned sternly, 'You go there, alone.'

Someone left the zebra's cage open in the zoo one night and he ran away to a local farm.

Early the next morning, he approached an old hen, saying, 'What do you do around here?'

The hen replied, 'I lay eggs for the farmer.'

The zebra then walked over to the cow, asking, 'What do you do?'

The cow replied, 'I give milk to the farmer.'

The zebra then spied an enormous bull and asked the same question.

The bull looked at the zebra quizzically and said: 'Listen, you queer ass, take off those faggy pyjamas and I'll show you what I do around here.'

The tall blonde model told the clerk: 'I don't know the style or colour of shoes, but I want low heels.'

The clerk asked, 'To wear with what?'

She said, 'A short, plump, elderly dress manufacturer.'

A tall, two-hundred-pound Texan, who was a loud braggart, died suddenly of a heart attack. At the funeral services his friends were surprised to note the small size of the coffin.

'That can't be what's left of Big Tom Gallagher,' said one of his friends.

'Sure it is!' replied another mourner. 'They simply let the bullshit out of him.'

One of the local islanders had had eight children in eight years. The doctor told him that he had to wear a sheath, explaining that as long as he wore it his woman could not have another baby.

A month later, the wife came in pregnant. The doctor got very angry. He called the man in and gave him a long lecture through an interpreter. He asked the man why he hadn't worn the sheath. The interpreter said, 'He swears he did wear it. He never took it off.'

The doctor shook his head. 'In that case, ask him how in hell his wife is pregnant again?'

'He says,' said the interpreter, 'that after six days he had to piss so badly that he cut the end off.'

An Englishman, a Pole and a Puerto Rican were standing atop the Empire State building, bemoaning their respective fates. Disgusted with their lives the three formed a suicide pact.

The Briton jumped first, sailing neatly to his doom . . . the Pole got lost on the way down . . . and the Puerto Rican stopped every few floors to scribble 'Fuck you!' on the walls.

Frank and Ronald – a married-without-benefit-of-clergy homosexual couple – had been spending a quiet evening at home.

'Hey, Ronald,' Frank called out, 'has the paper boy come yet?'

'Not yet, but he's getting a glassy look in his eyes.'

Two soldiers were canvassing the streets in a new town when a girl popped out of a doorway and cried: 'Hey, fellows, come on in and I'll give you something you've never had before.'

One soldier grabbed the other's arm and said, 'Let's get the hell out of here. She's got leprosy.'

Theresa and Jerry shacked up in a barn during a rainstorm. The screwing was so good that they decided to stay the night.

The next morning the farmer heard the commotion in the hayloft and entered his barn shouting, 'What's going on in here?'

'We're living on the fruits of love,' yelled Jerry.

'Well you better stop soon,' said the farmer. 'The skins are killing my chickens.'

A Pole was suffering from constipation, so his doctor prescribed suppositories.

A week later the Pole complained to the doctor that they didn't produce the desired results.

'Have you been taking them regularly?' the doctor asked.

'What do you think I've been doing,' the Pole said, 'shoving them up my ass?'

So this travelling salesman got an audience with the Pope.

'Hey, Father,' he said. 'Have you heard the joke about the two Polacks who –'

'My son,' the Pope said. 'I'm Polish.'

The salesman thought for a minute. 'That's okay, Father,' he said. 'I'll tell it very slowly.'

Two girls were comparing their experiences at the company's annual Christmas party.

'Did you get laid, Helen?'

'Twice.'

'Only twice?'

'Yeah, once by the band and once by the roadies.'

The recently married bride was perplexed when her husband announced that he had found a new position.

'What's that, honey?'

'We lie back to back.'

'But, what kind of position is that?'

'You'll see. Another couple is joining us.'

My friend was telling a pal that he had a dream that he was alone in a boat with Dolly Parton. His pal asked, 'Really, how did you make out?' My friend said, 'Great, I caught a twelve-pound bass.'